A Little Book About **Me** and my Dad

Illustrated by Jedda Robaard

This is a book to fill in and share with your dad.
You may need some help to complete it — that's what dads are for!
You can use the pouch in the back of the book to store photographs,
postcards, birthday cards, and anything else that is special to you and your dad.
Write a special message for your dad in the gift card provided.

First Edition for North America published in 2014
by Barron's Educational Series, Inc.

Copyright © The Five Mile Press Pty Ltd, 2013
Illustrations © Jedda Robaard

First published in 2013 by
The Five Mile Press Pty Ltd
1 Centre Road, Scoresby
Victoria 3179 Australia
www.fivemile.com.au
Part of the Bonnier Publishing Group
www.bonnierpublishing.com

All inquiries should be addressed to:
Barron's Educational Series, Inc.
250 Wireless Boulevard
Hauppauge, NY 11788
www.barronseduc.com

ISBN: 978-0-7641-6672-3

Library of Congress Control No.: 2013949686

Date of Manufacture: November 2013
Manufactured by: Leo Paper Products Ltd, Kowloon, Hong Kong, China.

Product conforms to all applicable CPSC and CPSIA 2008 standards.
No lead or phthalate hazard.

Printed in China
9 8 7 6 5 4 3 2 1

This is my
dad and me.

Draw or attach a photo of you and your dad here.

Mark these places
on the map.

I live in

...CALIFORNIA........

My **dad's** dad

is named

....

He is my grandpa!

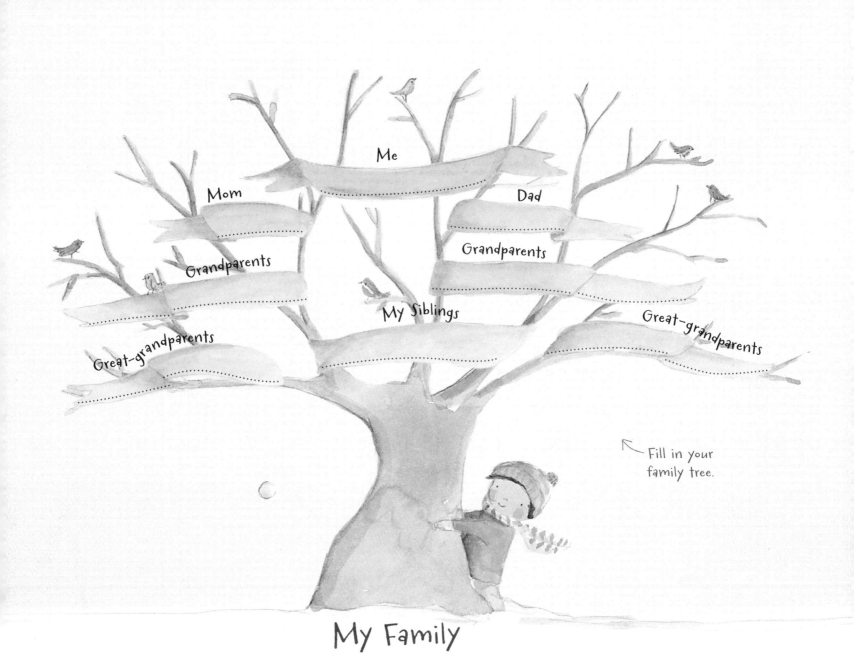

Me

Mom

Dad

Grandparents

Grandparents

My Siblings

Great-grandparents

Great-grandparents

Fill in your
family tree.

My Family

When Dad was little,

his favorite sport was ....

Now his favorite sport is ....

My favorite sport is .... Socar and football ....

.... Here is a picture of us playing together

When Dad was young,

his favorite game was

Pokemon ?

Draw a picture of your favorite game here.

My favorite game is

...Pokemon on 3DS...........

Dad and I love playing different games.

Our favorite games to play together are:

.....Monopily.................

.....Sonik all stars tranform

.....Sorry...................

.....One....................

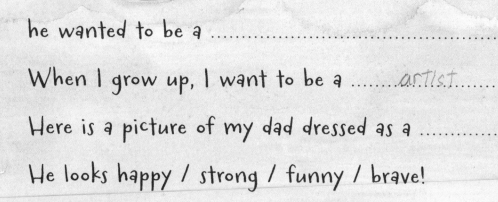

When Dad was my age,

he wanted to be a ....

When I grow up, I want to be a ....*artist*..

Here is a picture of my dad dressed as a ....

He looks happy / strong / funny / brave!

Draw a costume on Dad.

When
Dad
was
young,

his favorite music was

....

....

....

Now he likes to listen to

....

....

My favorite music is

Dad's
favorite
color is
...black.,,,.gra.....wight.................

My favorite color is

.........red, orange.........................

Color in the birds.

Here are some birds in our favorite colors

Dad and I love to make things in the kitchen

Dad's best recipe is

....

Our favorite thing
to eat is

................*meat*..........................

Make a list or draw your favorite foods here.

meat

brocily

carits

rice

pizza

black noodals

bense

peruvian groen
noodels

pasole

boretoes

tortec bene sape

carn

ticos

My dad
loves going
on vacations.

His favorite vacation was

Lake tahoe

He has always wanted to go to

the snow

The best place dad and I have been together is

Lake tahoe

Draw or attach a photo of you ↗
and your dad on vacation.

For my birthday,
Dad
likes to take me to the

....

The best thing we have done on my birthday is

....

My favorite birthday present from dad was

....

I love my dad

That's why I've made this special
book and card just for him!